OUTLAWS
RENEGADES
and SAINTS

OUTLAWS
RENEGADES
and SAINTS

DIARY OF A MIXED-UP HALFBREED

Tiffany Midge

GREENFIELD REVIEW PRESS

Publication of this book has been made possible, in part, through a Literary Publishing Grant from the Literature Program of the New York State Council on the Arts.

Outlaws, Renegades & Saints
Diary of a Mixed-Up Halfbreed by Tiffany Midge

Poems and Prose by Tiffany Midge

ISBN 0-912678-93-3

Library of Congress Number: 96-075513

Cover Art—Buffalo Bill Historical Museum

Design and composition of cover and text by Sans Serif Inc., Ann Arbor, MI
Printed by
The Greenfield Review Press
Greenfield Center, New York 12833

Distributed by The Talman Company, Inc.
131 Spring St.
New York, NY 10012

For my Trioux, Blioux, Sioux mother
Alita Rose

and for my wise-of-heart-and-spirit sister,
Julie Lynn

CONTENTS

1. Pieces of Glass Resembling a Human Heart

Spare Change   3
The Running Boy   12
Alice & The Engine That Could   13
Alice & Aurora Borealis   14
Alice In Spiderland   15
Fort Peck Indian Reservation   17
Mt. Rushmore & The Arm Of Crazy Horse   18
Ode To The Horse Powered Engine   19
Written In Blood   24
Totem Ad   25
Weeds   26

2. Nuclear Fission & the American Dream

Diary Of A Mixed-Up Halfbreed   31
Cowboys & Indians   44
Renegade Hearts   45
For Ransom   46
Mercy Killing   47
Travel Diary   48

3. Trail of the Outlaw's Tears

1-900-Deliver Me   59
Highway Robbery   63
Rodeo Queen   74
Outlaws, Renegades & Saints   76
Even the Outlaws Daughter Get's The Blues   78
Reward   88

4. The Reflection of Reluctant Saints

She Speaks Her Many Tongues   91
Saints   93
Iron Eyes Cody   96
Godless Nights & Firewater   97
Recipe For Survival   98
The Poet As Messiah   100
Night Of The Living Dead   101

ACKNOWLEDGMENTS

I owe a debt of gratitude and acknowledgment to the kind and loving support of K. Margaret, who offered me generous counsel and encouragement from the very beginning. I also wish to thank Elizabeth Baker, my co-worker and friend, whose steady guidance and daily affirmation broadened my vision and helped me to recognize my place in the world. Also special thanks to The Native Writer's Circle of the Americas and the Greenfield Review Press for their support in the making of this book. And for all the wonderful people I've come to know in the beautiful Northwest and counties beyond, thank you for your enduring commitments in making the world a better place.

Poems from this collection appeared originally in *The Ark, Blue Mesa Review, Cutbank, Durable Breath; Anthology of Contemporary Native American Poetry, Gatherings VI; En'owkin Journal of First North American Peoples, Metro Arts, The Raven Chronicles, Seattle Arts,* and *Weber Studies.*

INTRODUCTION

Tiffany Midge's *Outlaws, Renegades & Saints; Diary of a Mixed-Up Halfbreed* is a wildly irreverent book that boils up wit and anger into a heady stew to feed people who have been choking on romantic images of American Indians. If a reader agrees with Judson Jerome that, "Poetry should comfort the afflicted and afflict the comfortable," then that reader will find sustenance at this table.

Midge uses language in a variety of innovative ways in her work. She is a master of the prose poem, but at times can play with rhyme, rhythm, and repetition as intensely as a rap artist. She is a master at making extended metaphors reveal the emotional climate of a conflicted world. Often, her work pokes fun at the ways western culture, in general, and commercial culture, in particular, appropriates from indigenous people. She plays with product names and symbols making it clear how the stereotypes turn reality into parody, and she can turn that parody into a linguistic weapon to defend herself even when it wounds the user. Several of these poems make one laugh so hard one wants to cry.

Above all, Midge's work is personal; it investigates intimate moments and explores a point of view that is born of unique experience perceived from a singular perspective. These pieces talk of relatives, friends, her parent's failing marriage, of struggles to communicate across differences of culture in a racist world that is seldom comfortable.

In a series of linked works like her opening one about Grandpa Dick, Midge can weave the unique details of people's lives into a web that winds reality in gossamer strands that won't let go of the reader's imagination. Tiffany Midge opens a window on her particular world and, in doing so, reveals startling things about the human condition that everyone needs to know. The writing of this book waits for readers who understand that nothing and everything is simple. It is a pleasure to introduce such complex and risk taking work. Read on; this writing waits to be taken in.

Gail Tremblay
Olympia, Washington
August 1995

ONE

Pieces of Glass
Resembling a
Human Heart

Spare Change

—Brother, can you spare a dime?

1.

Grandpa Dick harbored pieces
of shiny silver in the bottom
drawer of his bedroom dresser.
Abandoned bits of fool's gold—
   forbidden.
Hidden beneath a leather antique flask,
yellowed love letters from Eliza
and a stale dream sandwich. We
discovered more than coin souvenirs,
claimed more than precious metals
but something even more valuable—
   secrets.
Day by day we stole them,
one secret at a time,
we stole them, thieves
creeping into his room,
looking for fat gold,
looking for thin promises,
looking for articles of the unknown,
prying our greedy palms—
   open
on the treasures that lay inside.

2.

The old Indian man who came to live with us, the old Indian man we called Grandpa Dick, always claimed to be rich. We didn't know any rich people and couldn't begin to even imagine that the old man with the tattered clothes and rotted teeth was a rich and wealthy man of means. A man of silver and gold. A man of promises. A man who owned a herd of horses. A man who believed in anything and everything all at once—because from him we learned that if you believed—because from him we learned that if you believed then anything, *anything* could happen. But only when you weren't expecting it, which is the hardest kind of belief to own. After Eliza was killed in a head-on collision, he continued to believe. After his only daughter married a white man and moved far far away from the reservation forever, he continued to believe. After his leg was taken away by hospital surgeons, he continued to believe. After we stole his secret treasures and bartered them for candy and comic books, he continued to believe. He always claimed to be rich, a wealthy man of means and we never believed him—we failed in our own belief. Years and years later, after my parents split for good, after the water heater broke down, after the car wouldn't start, after the furnace needed repair, after the dryer finally dried its last missing sock, after we were existing on nothing—existing on nothing but broken promises and stale powerless dreams, desperate to find anything—desperate to find anything to believe in, we received a check from the BIA for fifty-thousand dollars. That night my mother heard Grandpa Dick singing Dakota songs from the darkness of her closet. He was rich after-all. He'd owned oil-leased land in Montana and we were his heirs. He left us more than money, more than silver and gold, more than a bounty of delivered promises. He left us something to believe in. *Ourselves.*

4

3.

Grandpa Dick told us a story
   about the first man he ever killed—
the first white man he ever
   killed—that is. *He was just a boy*

then sittin' around drinkin' sweet wine in the Catholic
Church—Saint Mary's Church it was called then—with a
bunch of my wise-assed Indin friends and a skinny white
boy who liked to talk big but probably was afraid of his own
shadow, but wouldn't let anyone get the best of him, 'spe-
cially a small band of crazy injuns, who secretly he thought
himself better than. The church was nestled right-smack-
dab in the middle of the Catholic cemetery, not the Indin
cemetery at Chelsea, five miles out'a town toward Wolf
Point, but the apple cemetery, the place where the true be-
lievers lay to rest. Now doncha laugh when I tell you this,
but it really was a dark and stormy night and you could
hear wolves howling far off in the hills, only on that night
they sounded more like dead saints up to no good—and
there was a full moon covered by dark angry clouds and the
rain fell in steady good enuf bursts and we was all drinkin'
this sweet wine see—and all of us pretty drunk, not falling
down drunk but drunk enuf so that every nerve was charged
and alive and we were young and stupid but didn't know
enuf to know it. So anyway, this skinny white boy who
talked so big like he wasn't afraid of nuthin'—even go so far
as to hang with a rotten crowd of dirty injuns like us, just to
show he was better at being bad than at being good—pissed
off at his white daddy or something—I dunno—but anyway,
we was sittin' in that church and he was talkin' brave, that's
what we called him, Mr. Talkin' Brave, and Charles Big
Horse says, 'I'll give you twenty-five dollars if you take this
knife and go out to the big cross, ya-know that big cross
next to the alabaster statue of Mary, and pierce that cross
with this here knife, right in the middle, and tomorrow I'll
give you twenty-five dollars.' Well that guy said that he

5

wasn't afraid of nuthin' and that it sure was an easy twenty-five dollars and hell-yes he'd do it! So he went out into the darkness and the rain and it was an awful scary kind of night and he really did have a lot of nerve doin' that, and we was all laughin' when he left, cuz we all knew that Charles Big Horse sure didn't have no twenty-five dollars and even if he did, he'd never give it away to some skinny white boy who was trying to prove he was some kind of warrior. And that boy left and never did come back, but we just supposed that he chickened out and went on home. But the next mornin' nobody saw him around. So we all went back to that cemetery and that's when we found out he didn't make it home. Unless you consider goin' to the great beyond goin' home. He was sittin' next to that cross wearin' an expression you'd only imagine in your worst nightmares. And sure enuf that knife was stuck through the center of that cross just where we told him to put it. Only the knife was stuck through his overcoat too. We figured that the wind was blowin' so hard, blowing everything all over the place, that when he reached to stick the knife into the cross, he stuck the knife through his overcoat too without even knowing, and when he turned back around to leave, he felt something holding him back—felt something or someone pulling h.m back—and died right then and there of a heart attack. Died right then and there of fright. Scared to death takes on a whole new meaning. And I'll be damned if Charles Big Horse didn't scrounge up that twenty-five dollars and stuff it in that white boy's seer-sucker-suit-pocket when he was lay-ing out in his coffin at the funeral. All twenty-five dollars in Indin head nickels! Whoever said you can't take it with you was a damn fool, and what's more that boy was buried in the same cemetery he dropped dead of fright in! Now isn't that something?

6

4.

Our grandfather
never failed
each day
&
every day to rise
like the sun.
To rise
like a claimed promise
&
wind his way to the corner
tavern
spilling out memories of old & stale dreams,
pouring out years
of accumulated sorrows,
drinking up, drinking up, drinking up
generations of regret.
&
whatever change he had left
whatever change he had left
he never failed to deliver
his promise of chocolate
bars & tavern
popcorn.

5.

After Grandpa Dick lost his leg from a too-drunk stumbling/tumbling/mumbling fall on the gravel road leading to the neighborhood tavern—leading to the saloon of used-up/washed-out visions—leading to the gambling parlor of recycled wishes where thick-chested/lipsticked women forgave everyone's sins—no matter how dirty—they forgave you—forgave anyone. Even foolish old men swimming in tides of regret—spinning days through cheap tavern glasses/expensive tavern blues—falling/falling/falling down. *Don't we all eventually, inevitably all fall down?* Haven't we all sopped up our sorrows with the bread of too many failed dreams? And if we're lucky—and if we're lucky—doesn't the king's horsemen come and rescue us—come and save us from ourselves—from the inevitable decay we'll eventually become? Oh why does every lost-looking-old-man I see sitting broken on the city sidewalk have to look at me with my grandfather's eyes? Why is it that when I looked up the word *pathos* in my Random House College Dictionary, it said—*see Grandpa Dick.*

6.

After Grandpa Dick returned
    from the hospital
we asked him
    whether the doctors
used a saw
or a hatchet?

And would his leg be waiting for him
    in heaven
when he one day arrived?
    Mornings,
we'd burst into his room
    to watch him attach
his new leg
    to the place where his old
one was missing.

"Girls," he'd grin at us,
    *"Always make sure
you've got a spare."*

7.

I lose my first tooth. Jubilant I run to Grandpa Dick and hold up my bounty for him to see. It's then that I notice, I mean really notice, that he doesn't have any teeth. He tells me that he is a rich and wealthy man of means, sold his mouthful of teeth to the tooth fairy long ago and if I put my tooth underneath my pillow, the tooth fairy will leave me a treasure. I do just as he says only fight to stay awake so I can catch a glimpse of this promise. But the tooth fairy never comes. Instead, I watch as the sandman enters the room small as a piece of dust and rubs a Q-tip in the eye of my sleeping sister. Later, I searched for riches, or even small change but the sandman, he only leaves promises. I still have my first lost tooth. I keep it as a treasure.

8.

The old black & white
    TV kept our grandfather
from escaping into the deep
    pocket of himself.
When Neil Armstrong
    planted the red, white
& blue on the sprawling
    granite of the moon
Grandfather said, *"Look*
    girls, another whiteman
who thinks he owns it all!"
    When Iron Eyes Cody
filled the screen with his acid-
    rain-water eyes, Grandfather
said, *"Look girls, now*
    whiteman wants the Indin
to save 'em!" When heaps
    of anti-war demonstrators
flung daisies at the modern
    day bluecoats called *pigs*
Grandfather said, *"Look*
    girls, all these people
dressed up like warriors
    fighting against the war!"
His TV commentaries changed us,
    his TV commentaries changed us,
his TV commentaries changed us
    & we were spared
we were spared
    we were spared.

The Running Boy

Past the silent house windows,
pent-up regret creaking the gates
of the storekeeper's property,

past the waking black sky
shadowed by groaning clouds,

past ten o'clock curfew, the reservation
siren shrieks signaling our flight home.

Cousin Jimmy warns me to run
faster than I've ever run before—
You have to outrace the cop's bullets,
run before they see you!

I follow one-hundred yards/years behind him.
My lungs tangle against the dust,
draw escape like a deer's panic,
dull aches/quick beats of my heart
fold the night's curtain.

Jimmy knows this path/past—
its trail of memory sewn along the curve of his feet.
The running Indian boy remembers,

old escapes/past flights/soles flying
through the prairie wind,
past the gunfire
past the bellows/grunts/warnings of white soldiers.

He runs to remember.
He runs to forget.

Alice & The Engine That Could

Tired of being the passenger her whole life,
Alice Brought Plenty scouts the want-ads
in the Sunday paper for bargains & values.
Something with 4 wheels capable of delivering
the future more swiftly. She secretly
wishes for a machine of raw speed,
jet fueled & dream generated.

'89 Cherokee Chief, exc cond, V6, all pwr loaded, $5,100
'71 Cheyenne, half-ton, V8, nice cond, dependable, $2,500
'90 Comanche sport truck, white, great cond, $7,500
'90 Dodge Dakota 4x4, bright red, hurry won't last, $11,400
'90 Navajo LX-26, pwr pkg, good runner, $18,000

Alice thinks she could really fly in engines like these.
More than anything
she wants to transform
shotgun highways to magnum steel strips
engraved with her name.
With this kind of acceleration,
with this kind of power,
she could claim the future—
steal the red dust of every moment
by selling her past.

Alice & Aurora Borealis

Alice Brought Plenty considers the legends told by her grandmothers of Aurora Borealis appearing when star-maidens & sky-warriors are busy making love & creating new star children. This she would like to believe, though legends are of the past & the past is a Hallmark card postmarked galaxies away. Instead she compromises somewhere between science & myth. She assumes this belief will deliver her wishes unbroken, her dreams recovered. Alice spends her nights interpreting barely visible planets. She will not reveal the intentions of stars, will not forsake the confidence of constellations. She harvests hope through the telescope's eye & dispenses stars like pills to cure the bad dreams her head coughs out during sleep. Her mind is a grand room viewing a grand room & her solitary nights remain as testimony to the unimaginable distance of stars.

Alice In Spiderland

—For Iktome

It was famous doctor Freud who asserted that spiders are the unconscious' symbol for vaginas. I wonder if this is a rationale for my gay friend Richard who just about passes out at the sight of one.

***

A lover leaves me; his departing *Movie-Of-The-Week* line, "You're a spider, I'm a fly in the web you've woven, you'll trap me, suck me dry and never let go."

***

I'm 9 and spending every summer afternoon hunting bugs and sticking them to all the webs I've found just to watch the spiders wrap my gifts with silk.

***

At age 7, I encounter a cyclops spider, its body as big as my father's fist. Its giant red eye opened from the center of its body, blinked once then closed again, the movement of a slow motion movie projector, *click . . . click . . . click . . .* I run like hell or from hell whichever comes first.

***

Father takes the family to Mexico. Under the bed in the beach house cabin he's rented, a baby black widow recovers from my mother's screams.

***

15

I'm 10. I cry when Wilber cries because Charlotte just died. But then I clap because Charlotte left a legacy of teeny spiders for Wilber to talk to.

***

Daddy-long-legs are the tamest of spiders. In the white house on Duvall Main we lived with so many of them, they practically tucked us into bed at night.

***

In my apartment, an arachnoid creature is entombed in the kitchen dome light. But I don't bother to rescue it. It'll have to wait until the bulb burns out.

***

I go to Ruby Montana's during lunch-hour and purchase a generous amount of plastic black spiders. I place them on cobwebbed wreaths for the office's Halloween decor. Brenda borrows one for her hair and I save one for Seymour Bones, the office's skeleton mascot.

***

If I wanted, I could buy a tarantula at the exotic pet store in Pike Place Market for 99.99. Another large species without the mildly poisonous venom and just as big and hairy, for a mere 19.99.

***

An acquaintance, Steena Vommet, who dances downtown at the Lusty Lady has giant purple spiders tattoed on her back to match her hair.

***

Have you ever rescued a spider from the bathtub at 3 in the morning, because at that late hour who knows what powers it might possess?

Fort Peck Indian Reservation

July, the month I caught
     the spirit of Poplar's centennial,
1992, the year our America recognized
     a quincentennial of an invasion,
the beginning to broken treaties
     and broken lives,
a red, white and blue day
     complete with fireworks
and plenty of barbecued beef
     commemorating a colonial
victory, is it true then,
     bad luck comes in threes
or was I too busy collecting
     Polaroids of Indian men
dancing through hoops
     leaping to drums
moving through imagined tall grass
     to notice the absurdity
of the particular day
     and all the unspeakable horrors
that led me along this path
     to this particular powwow
taking place on Fort
     Peck Agency's land.

Mt. Rushmore &
The Arm Of Crazy Horse

I remember the view. 4 carved faces
fleshed out from the granite of those sacred hills.

I don't remember knowing what I know now,
only my childmind's awe & curious disbelief

at the stone-white faces cut out from the horizon
more massive than any god I could imagine.

Trapped within another mountain, a warrior's
arm pointed toward battle, exhibited a simpler

truth, clearer than any white colonial freedom fighter
could tell me. And when I think about it,

without stepping on a soap box, without screaming
at my conservative amway-loving friends,

without purchasing dynamite or spray paint,
that arm slowly sculpted into view, should have remained

just an arm—attached to a hand pointed toward
battle. Just an unfinished tribute to an unfinished war.

Ode to the Horse Powered Engine

*"If one were only an Indian, instantly alert, and
on a racing horse, leaning against the wind, kept
on quivering jerkily over the quivering ground,
until one shed one's spurs, for there needed no
spurs, threw away the reins, for there needed no
reins, and hardly saw that the land before one was
a smoothly shorn heath when horse's neck and
head would be already gone."*
—*The Wish to be a Red Indian*, Franz Kafka

1.

Before chrome pistons, crank-shafts and cruise control,
there were stallions, palominos, pintos and ponies.
Before asphalt, car-pool lanes and expressways,
there were wide-open plains, prairies and sage-bowl
landscapes. Somebody's vision of power
was ignited, a new mode of transport was bred
and a future designed by genius was born.

2.

My family used to live next door to a junkyard
guarded by a fierce German-shepherd named Puppet.
It was strewn with the motor innards of dead cars,
a trash heap of failed metal organs and stale powerless
dreams. Beyond the junkyard was a field of horses—
they stood all day grazing on buttercups, meadow grass
and crab apples fallen from nearby trees.

19

Beauty raced with them—bodies the carved
muscles of a god's extravagant whim,
magnificent packaged flesh of a vision gone to pasture.

3.

i want to believe
the plains indians invented horses
that somehow
those herds of sprinting hooves
were created
by the medicine of some warrior's nightmare some holy man's
vision of tomorrow
no—i need to believe it

4.

Once upon a time I dreamt of traveling with a caravan
of mystic gypsies who loved spun gold, red wine
and laughter. Nights I would find them
in a furious whirl of dancing and singing.
Their wagons were pulled by a herd of proud centaurs.
One was fair with the face of a Roman statue.
Another was fiery black with African features.
After everyone went to sleep—I stole them.

5.

Last March I purchased a car.
The auto dealer wore thick gold chains
and grinned at me with broken and missing teeth.
He sold discarded engines, snake oil and firewater.
Revving the motor of a Dodge Colt
I heard the roar of 800 horses trafficking
across dust and ash, arriving to the other side of eternity.

Got a lot of power, this one! Said the man
with the chrome-plated eyes.
Next, he showed me a Ford Mustang
except the engine refused to turn over.
All I could hear was the echo of drums
beating against the generator.
Finally, I drove home in an Escort Pony—
we bartered and made a good trade.
The engine still runs,
but I could have had something more powerful
I could have had a V-8.

6.

Driving to the park-and-ride on weekday mornings,
I am greeted by herds of horse powered engines
grazing on asphalt in the parking lot.
One morning I find that the herd has vanished
and are replaced with Zulu trucks
and Masai sports sedans. On the 6:00 news
a coalition of outraged consumers and civil
rights activists are suing the auto industry.
They win. *I don't know if I should laugh or cry.*

7.

some nights
i am shaken to consciousness
by turning dust
hoof prints lay scattered
across my bed
the now bare room
of my vision
reveals ghosts of equestrian
soldiers decorated
in sashes of scarlet
and helmets of frozen blue wind

their words are electric
forcing my will to surrender
from this nightmare
some dreams
you never wake up from

8.

Some saying used to go—*you are what you eat.*
Now I hear—*you are what you drive.* This is the way
I'll explain to my children the definition of irony.

9.

The monster truck rally
is coming to the Kingdome.
That same weekend
the gay rodeo is happening in Enumclaw—
queers on steers
the posters read.

I can't decide which to attend
so I stay home and watch the 6:00 news—
a story is being broadcasted

about crowds of demonstrators
and animal rights activists
opposing the gay rodeo—

one guy complains on camera
that the oppressed are oppressing—
I notice nobody is picketing the Kingdome.

10.

On the Ponderosa
Little Joe get's into a skirmish
with some horse thieves,
Hos and Adam
throw their two fists in the squabble—
the thieves go to jail
and the show has a happy ending.
I switch channels just in time
to watch Starsky and Hutch
apprehend a gangster
for organized grand theft auto,
the show has a happy ending.

I'm still waiting for a happy ending.

Written In Blood

I surrender to *Roget's Pocket Thesaurus*. I confess
my crime of breaking into this container of words
and slaughtering this poem with meta-innuendo.

But I needed something. I wanted to gather the dust
of more than three-hundred men, women and children.
I robbed from this vault of words,

language of the enemy, in hopes I could capture
these people, allow their prayers to reach
Wovoka in the final hour before I end this poem.

I wanted to know that I'm not grieving merely
from the guilt of that European blood that separates
me from two worlds. I need to know

that I can be allowed my grief. Sadly I have failed.
This nineteen-sixty-one *Cardinal Edition Thesaurus*
I depended upon has betrayed me. Betrayed

my Indian kin. With this language there are times
I feel I'm betraying myself. In my search
for synonyms for *murder,* I find *Cain,*

assassin, barbarian, gunman, brute,
hoodlum, killer, executioner, butcher,
savage, Apache, redskin.

Totem Ad

Wanted
spirit animal
no
tricksters
schemers
or sinners
no
heyokas
shaman posers
or cultists
must possess
infinite wisdom
courageous soul
with
sunny disposition
& intact open heart
winged creatures
need not apply
North American land animals
encouraged
water animals OK

Weeds

*—Weed 1.a. A plant considered undesirable,
unattractive, or troublesome, especially one
growing where it is not wanted, as in a garden.*
                                        —Webster's II

He was uprooted from his hometown bed,
transplanted to ours. Mother stocked the kitchen
cupboards with good intentions, placed store bought
flowers in the room he would sleep, began to hum
through the house in anticipation of the train

    delivering her widowed father,
    delivering her childhood hills,
    delivering her moist memories.

The house recovered from its stoic walls of oak and pine,
absorbed warm coals the furnace offered. With Mother
smiling our steps grew more certain, she allowed
the shades to disassemble and the windows to open.

Our grandfather fed us a rich diet of leather-bounded
bible stories, displayed toothless grins at his own jokes,
his tonic of reservation humor,
recited prayers in Sioux when we were sick.
Once acquainted with the town's businesses
he kept daily company at the Duvall Tavern,
returning with promised bags of popcorn and chocolate,
bottled sweet wine for himself—a medicine to be taken
before sleep, after the house sighed,
after the cat was put out—
he invited the night into his room,
his heart mushrooming against the dark.

Oh Eliza, Eliza, we rode those hills good,
our ponies were young and fast . . .
you were so beautiful, so beautiful.

He provided a reservoir during bad seasons—
offered solace to our witnesses when the night
grew teeth and venus flytrap jaws. We took
root in his arms then, burrowed in the velvet-lined
dugout, escaped the sting of tornado vines.

Eliza, tell these girls that Indians don't cry,
tell them their faces will fall off from salt
water and sadness.

Sometime between an October frost and a full eclipse
the floor beneath our bed rattled and shook,
starlight pointed through terrible shadows,
from another room our mother sent a scream
that ripened the morning, opened every flower.

Will you still think me handsome when I join
you in heaven? Will Peter open the gates and let
me enter, even though I am clumsy and foolish?

Mother drove everyday to the hospital. We stood
outside his room on tiptoes pressing our faces
against the glass, wondered if the doctors used a saw
or a hatchet, decided his leg went to heaven
to wait for him when he one day arrived.

He learned to walk by directing his weight
in the miraculous new limb. All was as it was before,
the gifts, wine, stories and solace. Nothing
had changed, except us. He had dragged our hearts
to an avenue we'd never crossed, a river never
before entered, we learned pity, we learned pathos.

Oh Eliza, I feel another in this room,
I smell lemon water and roses, I dream
of our hills, the starch of Mother's apron.

Mavis June drove from Poplar in an old rusted Chevy
with her boyfriend Amos Young Bull. They moved
into the utility room, rested their suitcases on the lid
of the washing machine, slept soundlessly on the fold-
out couch, turning their faces away from the light.

In the morning the house greeted us with emptiness,
and we didn't bother rising from our beds,
we knew he was gone. We knew he was gone
without saying goodbye. Father told us some folks
are like weeds, pull them out of their place,
they'll always return. Later we received a letter—

> *Dear Girls,*
> *The summer has turned out warm and beautiful.*
> *Come and visit me soon. Currants and chokecherries*
> *are almost ready. Eliza will make preserves and pies*
> *when you come. She sends her love. Be good.*
> *Love, Grandpa Dick*

Two

Nuclear Fission & the American Dream

Diary Of A Mixed-Up Halfbreed

January, 1966

My father pulled our family tree up by the roots and separated us into two separate halves. He and I staked a claim in the Pacific Northwest, colonized unfamiliar territory like any ambitious pioneer would. Using me for ransom he coerced my mother into signing a treaty that would cut clean her traditional ties to the Dakota lands she knew and loved. She and my half-sister relocated to the reservation of my father's design, surrendered to the prospect of his feverish schemes. We re-planted in a trailer park and waited for the dust to settle. The future didn't pan out the way my father expected. All we discovered was fool's gold.

February, 1967

They are fighting again. It's raining cats and dogs outside and they are fighting cowboys and Indians inside. I don't know which side to take, either way I'm branded a traitor or renegade. I have no loyalty for either side. All I can do is sit divided somewhere in the middle of their war and wait for this damn rain to stop. Wait for the thunder to break and the clouds to separate into two equal parts that don't add up to the confusion in my fractioned heart. Then, maybe the sun will come out and my parents will forgive the broken pieces of themselves.

March, 1968

i.

At the Oil-Celebration Powwow giveaways are the gift that keeps on giving.
The Indians true to their traditions continue
to give what the whites have taken from them.

ii.

food
when they were starving
blankets
when they were freezing
clothing
when they were naked

iii.

*Ethel Iron Thunder gives a Pendleton wrap to Minnie Spot-
ted Elk / Minnie Spotted Elk gives a star quilt to Silas Tail
Spins / Silas Tail Spins gives twenty lbs of frozen venison to
Victoria Walking Child / Victoria Walking Child gives a case
of chokecherry preserves to John & Myra Two Feathers /
John & Myra Two Feathers gives Cain Long Bow 100 dollars
towards his college tuition / Cain Long Bow gives Alice
Brought Plenty 10 yards of bargain basement fabric / Alice
Brought Plenty gives Ruby Savior a plastic bag of accumulated copenhagen chew top lids / Ruby Savior gives Mary &
Victor Red Wing a beaded cradleboard for their new arrival /
Mary & Victor Red Wing gives Scarlett Comes At Night their
family's secret frybread recipe / Scarlett Comes At Night
gives Ethel Iron Thunder insulated rabbit fur slippers and
matching blue mittens and scarf.*

iv.

Define Indian Giver in 10 words or less:
All of the above.

v.

Grandma Iron Thunder tells me
that giveaways are to Indians
what Christmas is to white people.

April, 1969

". . . they are fighting again"
—Walter Cronkite

They are fighting again. My plastic green soldiers are marching across the dense shag carpet capturing POW Fisher Price animals and GI Joe action figures. They are fighting again. Barbie and Skipper are taken hostage by Ken and drowned in the bathtub. They are fighting again. My black baby doll Tamu is tortured by the Velveteen Rabbit, her talking string gets stuck on one lonely phrase, sock it to me baby—sock it to me baby—sock it to me baby. They are fighting again. My Etch-a-Sketch draws a picture of military intelligentsia popping war buttons and planning strategic defenses. They are fighting again. The Brothers Grimm are cutting fillets of Hans Christian Andersen's little mermaid and choking the princess on her pea. They are fighting again. Betty and Veronica turn Jughead and Archie's top secret mission into Viet Cong headquarters. They are fighting again. All sixty-four Crayola Crayons grind the heads of the box of twenty-four in their built-in-sharpener, leaving no survivors. They are fighting again—they are fighting again—they are fighting again.

May, 1970

My father brings home a bundle hidden inside his sports coat. He tells me to guess what it is. I secretly wish that it's a monkey and that my father is the man-in-the-yellow-hat. But it isn't and neither is he. He opens his coat and a scruff of fur and teeth peeks out. It's a German Shepherd pup we name *Sunka* which means dog in Sioux. At dinnertime, Father jokes and tells us that mother cooked Sunka and that this is the scrawny meat cowering next to our cream corn. My sister begins to cry and my mother glares at my father as if to say, *you're not funny*. This is my father's version of Indin humor except nobody ever laughs. Later, we have to put Sunka to sleep. He fell in with the wrong crowd and was accused of killing sheep. So Father brings a mustard colored mutt home and we name it Custer. Father tells us that a mutt is your basic halfbreed, only nobody knows which side it's on. He smiles at me when he says this. Indin humor. Later, Custer was attacked by the junkyard dog, Puppet, who lives next door. All that was left of his yellow coat and dog-eyed expressions we'd come to adore was a greasy spot in the driveway where he was massacred. There was no trace of remains for us to bury. Indin justice.

June, 1971

My mother's nephew from her previous marriage drops in with his new wife and ends up staying longer than my father thinks is an appropriate amount of time. James and Ida have abandoned the reservation and want to make a new start in the big city ripe with opportunity. Ida brought along her dance costume and part of their newlywed plans of locating employment consists of her doing the Ladies Traditional at Washington State powwows. But she fails to captivate her judges. Her moccasinned feet carry too many years of regret and keep missing the end of the drum beat. My mother works at the personnel department at King County and sets up interviews for James. But he fails to show up, tells her—*I over-slept, I forgot, I didn't have gas money.* One morning I wake up to find a tent pitched in the back yard and a beat-up car five different shades of green parked in front of the house. James and Ida and their friends Carla and Piper are having a powwow under our apple tree. *Relatives or not, these good-for-nuthin'-dead-beats have got to go!* My father rages at my mother. *They've freeloaded long enough!* I'm sorry to see them go. Ida taught me how to inhale Salem 100s without choking to death. Carla plucked my eyebrows, said I was mature for my age. James let me drive his car up and down the suburban street in reverse. Piper gave me a can of beer, said *drink up half-pint.* Later, we received news that James was serving a life-term at Walla Walla for murdering a store proprietor and his wife. None of the relatives believed he was responsible. Being an inmate brought out James' warrior aptitude. He hung for half-an-hour with skewers sewed into his chest and received a vision that cleared the clouds and webs from his soul. He became a father during visiting hours when he and Ida practiced their religious beliefs in a sweat lodge ceremony. They named their baby Freedom.

37

July, 1972

It is my birthday. I ask my mother, *"when I grow up will I be a full-blooded Indian?"*

August, 1973

SHELLI: If you could have your choice, who would you marry Donny Osmond or David Cassidy?
ME: I can't decide I'm torn in two pieces.
SHELLI: Is Cher Bono really a halfbreed Cherokee Indian?
ME: No, one half is Cher and the other half is Sonny.
SHELLI: How can you be allergic to horses if you're Indian?
ME: How can you be so tactful if you're white?
SHELLI: Are your parents on welfare or do you get money from the BIA?
ME: Neither, my parents are AIM subversives infiltrating the FBI and the CIA undercover. Your father is under investigation.
SHELLI: If I gave you a present and then took it back, would that make me an Indian giver?
ME: No, it would make you an enemy.
SHELLI: So, you're part German and part Cherokee?
ME: Yeah, my father is German and my mother is a jeep.
SHELLI: No seriously, what are you?
ME: Part Irish and part Winnebago. My mother is Irish and my father is a motor home.
SHELLI: Why are you confusing me—now I'm all mixed-up!
ME: Right, that makes two of us. Now do you understand?

September, 1974

My parents split like atoms in a nuclear, free testing zone, finally exploded then walked around for the next few years trying to recover the lost parts of themselves. They choked on words like *love* in a household strewn with radiation fall-out. Mother began serving mammoth garden vegetables, mutated from all the toxicity refuging in the kitchen cupboards. My father didn't speak for a year. All the houseplants died. Poisonous mushrooms grew rampant and out of control in the living room. Venomous spiders and snakes crawled and slithered up the walls. This was no mild case of the deetees. This was divorce. This was the aftershock from years of regret. Divorce pries every kid into two separate halves. Parents negotiate for the best parts. *Here, you take the left thigh, I'll take the right. You can have the teeth but don't expect me to pay for braces. If I give you a hand can I have the shoulder. Don't hog all its love, I get some too! No, wait give me its heart, here you take its mind. We'll divvy up the eyes, one for you and one for me OK? Careful you clumsy jerk you'll bruise it! I'll take the white half and you take the Indian half, then we'll each get what we started out with, agreed?* On weekend visitations, my father snaps at me in an even-measured tone— *you're really getting to be neurotic, just like your mother!* During the week my mother gets flustered, rolls her eyes in an exaggerated fashion and says—*you're selfish, just like your father!* My half-sister when we're playing monopoly, will draw an imaginary boundary between us, as if to say—*whose side are you on?* Years later, I will return to the house and its stoic walls of oak and pine. Only it's not a residence anymore but a meat house. The friendly neighborhood butcher allows me to wander in the old war zones. Each room opens a new wound. My parent's bedroom is the deep freeze. The living room is a slab of cutting board. The room I shared with my half-sister is a novelty gift parlor where visitors can purchase nail clippers, blackberry preserves, incense and greeting cards. When I finally leave, I'm in stitches.

October, 1975

It's Halloween night. This year more than anything, I want to be a real Indian. But my mother didn't have time to make me a costume, so I have to wear a billowing white sheet and go out as Casper the Friendly Ghost.

November, 1976

Its a Bicentennial Thanksgiving. Each day at school we're required to recite the Pledge of Allegiance and garnish our red-blooded American pride with offerings of thanks. I tell my classmates that *god* is *dog* spelled backwards and Mrs. Svenson keeps me after school for two-hundred years. I tell my classmates that *live* in *evil* spelled backwards and Mrs. Svenson makes me write it on the chalkboard two-hundred times. On the fateful turkey day, I'm surrounded by Indians adorned in construction paper war bonnets. Everyone is waiting for the cranberries I was assigned to bring to our class potlatch. *"I didn't forget, I just didn't bring them!"* Mrs. Svenson banishes me from the festivities and asks, *"Whose side are you on?"*

December, 1977

It's Christmas time. Mother decorates the house with tinsel, candycanes, holly leaves, pine boughs, ornaments, x-mas cards, reindeer, golden candles, bright red ribbons, dancing mice, twinkling lights, angel's hair, mistletoe, babies breath, and bowls of shelled nuts. The living room looks like Santa Clause vomited. We had to take the cat to the vet because he ate tinsel. It didn't snow. Father brought frog-legs and caviar hor- d'oeuvres. The chestnuts burned. Grandpa fell off the roof. All the chocolate santas on the tree melted. Uncle Dwight got drunk. My sister accidently put salt in the sugar cookies. Mother saw an owl sitting on the backyard picnic table. A big storm crashed into an electrical pole and all the lights went out. Christmas Eve we sat in the dark praying for a savior.

Cowboys & Indians

Inspired by John Wayne movies &
black & white episodes of Gunsmoke,
my father stayed true within the Montana
borders, scouting for a dream
he wanted to own forever. Only
dreams—sometimes they play crooked cards.

He staged his life harboring between
real experience & comic book action—
played summer-stock in Big Fork,
memorized lines written by Chekov,
re-named Flathead Lake,
watched scenes open in bottles
of Redeye & Rotgut,
close during piss-drunk fistfights.

The biggest role in his make-believe
cowboy life came when my mother
entered into it. Trouble was, he got stage
fright when performing for intimate crowds.
His fingers got itchy when surrounded
by his Indian in-laws & my Sioux cousins.

The bar room brawls he invited
choreographed themselves into our lives.
The Matt Dillon in our kitchen
wasn't no hero.
Just a guy with so many big ideas
they exploded like lady-pistols,
wrecked the soundstage.
During those starry starry nights
we learned to play dead.

Renegade Hearts

My parents fell fast, dropped hard. Their blood
young hearts elected to gamble, they wanted to take
fate by the horns, ride out their melodrama
and dreams of forever.
Together they stole a gold miner's claim,
harnessed each other's nickel plated ego,
endured in-law's pulpits, tempted every commandment.
Razor sharp tongues soon uncovered their myth.
Wanting to escape, my father kidnapped me to Seattle.
Attempting a treaty his warrior
soul held me for ransom.
At dawn the next day, my mother drove in from Montana,
sick with worry, resigned herself to answer
questions, give-in, defer
upon my father's requests. His alibi
angered her but she contained the stoic statue
within, left her tired words unsaid.
Minutes dissolved and the air formed granite truth,
a silent agreement was reached. Ennui
numbed them both to dead calm.

For Ransom

Over-taken by an adolescent whim,
my father stole me away into an August Montana night.
Burdened with bottles & blankets
we boarded a train
leaving foothills,
unsuspecting in-laws &
Mother behind. We moved
toward a point desperate
to be proven.

So many hours & miles passed
just to gain treaty.
Such deep roots pulled to calm nuptial disputes,
lay a path for Father's indulgence.

Weeks later, point taken,
we were all living in a pale pink trailer
surrounded by buttercup pasture,
guarded by high pines & cedars.

Secured by Boeing, Father worked,
Mother kept house, torn away
from her native limb & grieving
for the indigenous vaults of cornflowers & sagebrush.

Having paid the ransom price she could only hope
to someday embrace the strange
green atmosphere,
wrap her daughters in the new foliage
made comfortable
by her resolve.

Mercy Killing

My scientific father's sympathy
for creatures in pain introduced itself
to me along a water's edge
where a mallard duck sat in a nest
of blood-stained sand.

I had my first anatomy lesson
before I even reached my father's buckle.
The wounded bird just sat, its last flight
only a memory, its black eyes

dull, carrying
a blank stare creatures have when in pain.
Down crashed Father's axe.
Blood splayed, my skin jumped,
another lift of the axe

and no longer was there a suffering
duck but a specimen.
Father's axe was as sharp
as his curiosity and he showed me
the transparent bubble and said,
this is how it floats.
I looked up into my father's face,
a mortal god, and let my eyes
rest back to the bird.
Just the bubble remained
sticking up from some feathers the shore
wind hadn't blown away.
I searched for my mother.
She stood watching from down shore.

Her eyes told a story of what creatures
do when they are in pain.

Travel Diary

Day 1.

There are no travel brochures for the reservation vacation. No glossy posters and prints depicting pairs of Indian lovers intertwined along the concrete shores of the Fort Peck Dam. There's no 1-800 numbers to call ahead and secure reservations, consider yourself already booked. The only travel agency you'll want to contact is the tribal one at the edge of town. They'll ensure that you belong, that your stay is comfortable, that you'll return home refreshed. If you want they'll even offer to enroll you—issue you a photo ID. If you don't fully qualify as a member of the tribe, they'll refer you to other bands that are advertising—maybe you could roadie.

Day 2.

It's July the 4th, 1992. Poplar is celebrating its Centennial. I can't remember if the old saying goes, *good luck comes in threes,* or if it's, *bad luck goes in threes.* Either way this town has opened every window, shaken out the rugs and hung out every piece of laundry on the line. Downtown is a regular 3-ring circus. Crepe paper floats are sailing through mainstreet carrying 500 years of forgiveness, 216 years of red-blooded American pride and 100 years of a prospector's wet dream. Smokie the bear is lumbering behind a Dodge Dakota 4x4 filled with buffalo robes and Indian princesses waving sparklers. The Poplar Junior High marching band is creeping behind the pioneer's horse drawn covered wagons to the tune of the motion picture theme song, *Eye of the Tiger.* The Fort Peck troop of Vietnam war vets are dodging the missives of Bozo the Clown's Tootsie Pop ambush. The Poplar High School pep squad is passing out their high kick rendition of spirit to a crowd of Japanese tourists wearing *Northern Exposure* T-shirts. The troop members of Desert Storm are being pursued by the ghosts from the 7th Cavalry who are topped with non-dairy Dream Whip. A John Deere tractor is pulling a tinfoil wrapped Santa Maria filled with evangelist missionaries treading behind a tragic clown's trail of tears. BIA agents in ten-gallon hats are dishing out miniature flags to a congregation of undercover AIM activist posing as nuns and cheerleaders. This evening I write a postcard to my co-workers. *Hey guys! Today I witnessed 500 years crammed into a mini-segment of 60 minutes. Andy Rooney would love this! After today, I know for sure that the melting pot is definitely melting, perhaps we should recycle it and repair the liberty bell. Having a wonderful time, wish you were here—Love, Tiffany*

Day 3.

Blue Reservation mornings

I am recovered by sobbing explosions, whiny country chords of Garth Brooks which Cousin Cookie has detonated in the living-room. She keeps the volume at maximum while she pieces together star-quilts or restores rodeo-dud-fabric in her yellow sewing room down the hall. An expert seamstress, she handiworks the prom gowns for the female student body at Poplar High. She draws her own patterns, designs her own rhythms. You could give her any page from the formal section in the Sears Catalogue and she'd sew it by heart. Her mind's eye is a charmed needle, her slim fingers remnants of stained satin or silk.

Blue Reservation nights

Alice Brought Plenty arrives to the house delivering years of regret. Her shoulders sag from balancing buckets of accumulated tears. Her mother's tears her grandmother's tears her sister's tears her own tears. Her broken heart is a country-and-western ballad ripped, mangled and torn beyond recognition. She throws the shards at Cookie's feet. Cookie gathers the fragments patiently, tenderly, as if she's collecting fragile and valuable pieces of glass. Alice stands waiting at the door while Cookie repairs her damaged heart. With surgical grace Cookie bastes the brittle splinters using her own regretful years as a guide. She stitches Alice's heart with strands of her grandmother's hair. The needles she uses are slivers of her children's bones. She knots the ends of the threads with mercy, with blood. The vessels are secure, the chambers sealed.

Pain cannot arrive if it hasn't a place to sleep.

Day 4.

Poplar is absent of grand casinos and gambling parlors. No golden palaces of chance to lay down your stakes and wager an accumulated lifetime of credit. But today, to commemorate the town's 100 years, the officials have designated a white rancher's field to compete with the riches and splendor of Las Vegas and the American Dream. The wide open throat of this acreage is painted with numbers, sectioned 5ft. by 5ft. until a government's *handout* purchased by a jolly rancher adopts the appearance of a casino's roulette board. Passenger-filled planes jetting over this crude design mistake eastern Montana as a holy shrine. The television newscasts preempt *Days of our Lives* to inform the American public that the Fort Peck Indian Reservation is now the center of miracles. TV evangelists and talk-show hosts begin speculating as to the significance of the sacred site. The National Inquirer wants to know god's motivation behind the divine conception. Cranks fill the circuits on syndicated radio waves. Eyewitnesses of the account sell their stories to the New York Times and the National Examiner. There is rumor that the Pope is coming, that the Pope is coming. An AP bulletin is issued to the defense department. The President assures the public that he is taking the matter under the advisement of the Capital and that in the meantime there is no need for alarm. Busloads of tourists come to the reservation to snap Polaroids and interview tribal elders. Somebody spotted Elvis eating Indin tacos. The government organized negotiations to trade the Black Hills for this newly discovered sacred shrine. Jane Fonda donates millions to the American Indian Fund. Oliver Stone makes a movie, casts John Trudell in the lead. Mother Teresa abandons the leper colonies and commits her life's service to the North American Indians. Years later, the truth is finally revealed. The Holy Shrine is demoted to the Big Joke. Indin humor rocks and shakes the bellies of every human being on the planet. During an interview with Phil

Donahue, the rancher who once owned the plot of land is quoted as saying, *"It weren't no shrine, we was having us a cowchip lottery.* When asked, what's a cowchip lottery? The rancher replied, *"Everybody bets their lives on one square patch of land, the cattle are unloaded then everybody waits for nature to call. From the looks of things, I'd say everybody went home a winner."* The world explodes in laughter.

Day 5.

The rodeo got cancelled. None of the Indians wannabee cowboys this year. Somebody suggests a buffalo hunt, but then we remember all the buffalo are gone. Cookie invites everyone over to her digs to watch videos, but nobody wants to on-account-of everybody already knows the end of the movie. Silas Tail Spins says, "We could get drunk." But Thunderbird has lost its power. Gladys Everybody Talks About, advocates the entertainment value in a good round of gossip. But everyone already knows everyone else's business. Alice Brought Plenty suggests we have a powwow, but everyone says, "Been there, done that!" Victoria Walking Child says, "I could do everyone's tarot reading?" But everyone can already guess at their futures. Cain Long Bow says, "We could interview the elders and learn about our heritage?" But all the elders have retired to Florida. Ennui covers the most hopeful of days into a blanket of apathy. Nobody knows what to do. So we all go home and sleep for a good long time. Nobody dreams.

Day 6.

We drive out to South Dakota to view a national monument. A symbol of America's pride. I think of baseball, hotdogs, apple pie, Chevrolets, and a conquered people's dream that perished so violently to accommodate this uncertain present. A once magnificent past is reduced to Hallmark cards postmarked galaxies away. When we finally arrive, a band of Hell's Angels are attempting to make a monetary treaty with the motel desk clerk. But the desk clerk won't take their money. They offer him booze, firearms, women, gold. At first glance you can tell the desk clerk is no stranger to bribery, you can tell he's a subscriber to Pat Robertson and Jimmy Swaggart, you can tell that he is a man shrouded in a heavy coat of fear. Fear of spiders, fear of dust, fear of public restrooms, fear of his mother, fear of his children, fear of his own mortality. But especially fear of bikers, gypsies and Indians. Fear of anything that defies confinement. We turn around and leave just in time to hear the echo of breaking glass. We know it isn't Armageddon, but centuries of accumulated fear. We drive to the "shrine." Gutzon Borglum is captured in the rock immediately below Lincoln's heavy brows, as if to say, *justice is just but revenge is sweet.* Winnebago and Apache land cruisers are positioned randomly throughout the parking area, as if to say, *one man's shrine is another man's cemetery.* A bright ribbon of red paint is smeared across Washington's classic nose, as if to say, *goddamn, this elevation has given me a nosebleed.* Trapped within another mountain, several miles away, a warrior's arm is pointed towards the men's room, as if to say, *America is going to the toilet.* On our way out of Keystone, we stop at a souvenir shop. I can't resist buying the Indian bow, arrow and knife set, wrapped up in a slick package of artificial African leopard skin.

Day 7.

We arrive to Bullhead just in time to watch Evil Knivel make his infamous jump over the Snake River Canyon. I don't have the heart to tell my cousins that he failed this leap years ago and that the TV broadcast has only just now reached their antennae. Cousin Alfred bets everyone that Evil Knivel is really Elvis Presely staking out the territory of a new career. I hold back from informing him that Elvis is dead. There's no food in the house to eat, except inedible commodity, so Alfred, Penny, Trudi, Johnny, Liza and her friend all pile into my half-sister's Dodge Dakota 4x4 and we drive to the mercantile. Halfway out of the yard, Johnny screams savagely, *"You're dragging a dog, you're dragging a dog!"* My half-sister slams on her brakes, everybody is thrust forward, Johnny is laughing, *"Just fooling . . . aaay!"* At the mercantile, we pile up our purchases on the counter. 2 loaves of Wonder Bread, a case of Vienna Sausages, catsup, mustard, sweet rolls, milk, Kool-aid, bacon, 2 dozen eggs, 6 cartons of cigarettes and an apple. When we arrive back to the house, we're surrounded by Indians. Auntie Mugs spread the word that we are in town and will pay cash for commodity cheese. When we finally leave, she pulls my mother aside and asks if she could please mail her any extra VCRs.

Day 8.

Returning to Poplar in time for the Oil-Celebration Pow-wow, we meet up with my mother's childhood friend Patsy whose visiting from Vegas. Pulling up to the powwow grounds we're stopped by a young tribal officer. He searches the inside of the car with his flashlight. *"Are you carrying any alcohol?"* Patsy grins, leans out the window and shoots back, *"No, you got any?"* Everybody cracks up. Patsy reloads, *"Officer I'm clean but I don't know about my friend here, you should give her a strip-search, aaay!"* At the arena we buy cokes and frybread and claim a length of bleachers. The men's traditionals are wearing Ray Bands. The grass dancers are adorned in acres of yarn. The fancy dancers are kicking up their Adidas sneakers. The jingle dancers are chiming and clanging years of accumulated Copenhagen chew top lids. The shawl dancers are dancing circles around the hoop dancers. Somebody drops an eagle feather. All the whirling, buzzing, singing, swirling, bustling, drumming and frenzy abruptly stops to a dead calm. During this commercial break half the congregation gets up to search out the sani-cans. A solemn ceremony is presented. A tall Indian man with elk teeth dangling around his neck and deer antlers crowning his head, slowly marches to the center of the arena. Everyone watches, waits, listens to him offer a prayer to the spirits that preside. He shakes a tortoise rattle over his head to each of the four directions. He sings a holy song in a barely audible whisper. He leans down towards his moc-cosinned feet and tentively without haste, slow, slow, slowly, plucks the fallen feather from the sawdust as if he's recovering sharp glass amid water and graciously turns, returning it to its owner. The dancing resumes.

THREE
Trail of the Outlaw's Tears

1-900-Deliver Me

***

Glenda, my psychic friend from the psychic friend
hotline delivers a message
in cryptic detail—
a tree falls in the forest,
a woman in Iowa stirs lime flavored jello,
a schoolboy in France eggs a nun,
a thunderstorm breaks out in the Himalayas—
Three dollars a minute and all I get is static interference.

***

Browsing the yellow pages I came across a delivery
service promising redemption. I order a life to go with
pepperoni, olives and a happy ending. It's been well over
twenty years, and I'm still waiting.

***

The only thing I'm sure of is that I'm not sure of anything.
—Anything else?
Yes, someday you will probably die.
—Is that just another empty promise?
I'm not sure.

***

My life is an excerpt from *Waiting for Godot:* only more
surreal and more vague.

***

If you empty your mind, they will come.
Who will come?
If you open your heart, they will come.

Who will come?
If you forgive your enemies, they will come.
Who will come?
Please deposit a pint of blood and stay on the line.

***

The TV evangelist suggested I cleanse my soul, but I accidentally used too much bleach and now I have no hope of ever recovering it.

***

I placed an ad in the personal columns.
Wanted: Spirit Animal—
Coyote responded, said he was everything
I'd ever wanted and possibly more—
but later he confessed he was afraid
of making commitments.
Every animal I've ever known has been a trickster.

***

If I wanted I could walk the Red Road: only I keep getting hung up in traffic.

***

The medicine man told me that my totem was an eagle. You could say I purchased an Eagle Vision, fully loaded in 36 EZ installments.

***

"I found salvation in Thunderbird wine." The drunk at the
pier tells me.
"I woke up and saw the face of an angel." The nameless
woman cried.
"I looked to the grey grey sky and Christ was crying!"
Mavis June testified.
Is it possible to be blinded by a vision?

***

Sitting Bull was a Taurus. Custer was a Cancer. Glenda my psychic friend informs me that this is essentially the reason they didn't get along.

***

Shirley Maclaine answered my fan letter. I asked why it was that when the spirits appear to me, they are always laughing? She wrote back, that they were probably watching the re-runs of my life. How can I make them stop? I asked. Did you try switching channels?

***

At the annual powwow at Daybreak Star
I purchased a dream catcher from
Wasicu Indian Jewelry.
Minding the directions I hung
it over my bed
and have had nightmares
ever since.

***

Someone told me they bought a Plymouth Sundance. I asked why they hadn't purchased a Buick Baptism or a Ford Communion instead.

***

I wanted to write a letter to Galileo, only the Post Office refused to deliver it. But somehow I think he got the message because the next time I looked into the night's sky, I noticed the Big Dipper was shaped like a question mark.

***

Define irony in twenty words or less:
Irony is when an ice-princess and a proud Indian nation both carry on, in spite of wounded knees.

***

As the legend goes, Joan of Arc and Brown Weasel Woman both received visions from spirits to dress as men and prove themselves as warriors. The tragic difference, one found death in battle and the other was burned alive.

***

I couldn't make the monthly payments, so my Eagle Vision was re-possessed.

Highway Robbery

1.

Some crazy song is always playing on the radio at the precise moment the circumstances fit the occasion of the tune. Jung translates this to the phenomena of synchronicity. A recurring theme in my life. It's more than simple deja vu, it's more than prophetic dreams, it's more than finishing people's sentences. It's an associative adhesive gluing the fragments of the universe together. It's at these moments that Alice takes over the wheel and drives me straight into Wonderland. She's right on you know. The world denies no person the potential of awe. The potential of slamming the accelerator and delivering a future swifter than gunfire or thunder. The trick is, steering clear of the cliffs, rock slides and black ice. Steering clear of road kill, dead ends and roadside crosses. Tourist traps are inevitable on the nation's highways, and the tune playing on the radio is always the same. It could be Jim Morrison's *The End*, The Rolling Stones' *Under My Thumb*, or Muddy Water's *Rolling and Tumblin'*, but they're all the same song. They all spell out the same drumbeat and war cry. They all resonate the same intention. *Welcome to America, you've just entered the Twilight Zone.*

2.

Nearing twilight we pull up to Montana's 10,000 Silver Dollar restaurant, casino lounge and souvenir gift shop. I can't remember if the saying goes, *good luck comes in threes* or if it's *bad luck goes in threes*. But it doesn't matter anyway, because one look at this highway mirage and I'm struck with the reminding bolt that it sure was one hell of a lot of bad luck that it exists in the first place. A stoic wooden Indian greets us from the entrance as if to say, *tobacco is the Indian's timely revenge*. I wander the aisles of an entrepreneur's wet dream scouting for any evidence of justice. But all I can find is irony. *Irony*. I hold it in my hands like a valuable stone. I finger the point of its swift and sure intention. I caress the razor edge of its laughter. *Irony*. It's a sacrificial gem. *Irony*. It's my only defense. *Irony*. it's all we've been given. *Irony*. It's all we have left.

3.

Exit Next Left. We follow the sign's demand, arrive to our destination of departure and careen off the edge of the world falling to a fate unrouted and unchartered in a sea captain's log book. Our discovery came 500 years too late.

4.

Lord I'm one, Lord I'm two, Lord I'm three, Lord I'm four, Lord I'm five hundred miles away from home. We sang that song around spitting campfires and marshmallowed homogenized dreams one late spring at Camp Seabeck. We sang *Home of the Brave* on the drive up in a yellow checkered school bus with the only black student in the class orchestrating our voices. We sang *God Bless America*, covered our hearts with our hands and bellowed out the wrong words—*God bless my underwear, my only pair, through the washer through the dryer, through the toilet white with foam.* We sang *This Land is My Land, This Land is Your Land,* only our version was—*this land is my land, this land ain't your land, if you don't get off, I'll blow your head off.* Patriotism is wisdom spelled backwards. They never taught us that in elementary school. The most important lessons are self taught.

5.

Self-proclaimed shamans, plastic medicine men, Indian spirituality processed in K-mart variety packs. Messianic hysteria, wasp culture-crisis, altruistic snake oil salesmen peddling the wares of false prophets and seers. A woman I know tells me that she is an incarnation of an ancient Indian princess, she follows the vision of a Beverly Hills housewife who channels some thousand year old *shaman*. "Oh," I reply passively, "kind of like Ramtha in buckskins and beads huh?" She tells me of some other ancient soul who predicts California earthquakes and midwestern floods. "Oh," I reply apathetically, "kind of like Nostradomas with an almanac for a crystal ball huh?" She tells me that the hippie resurgence is proof that the Native Americans are the planet's saviors. "Oh," I reply indifferently, "kind of like the second coming in bell-bottoms and braids huh?" She tells me that she's traveled extensively through the spiritual highways of the ghost dancer's dreams. "Oh," I reply dispassionately, "did you have to make a reservation at the Holiday Inn?"

6.

While visiting in Oregon I stay with an old friend who I haven't seen for years. My first night there she takes me to a 13-steps-to-financial-independence-support-gathering, which is being held in the gymnasium of the local military academy. I can't escape the image of Tammy Faye Baker and Jim Jones in a revised version of *Invasion of the Body Snatchers*. A woman who looks like Jimmy Swaggart in stepford-wife drag, stands at the pulpit endorsing extra-strength, all-purpose, dish-cleaning, baby-oil, shampoo, car-wax, laxative, seltzer, spot-remover, shoe-polish, complexion-astringent, ear-wax-removal, window and laundry detergent. My friend who showed seven plans that week like a door-to-door Church of Latter Days Saint bike-peddler and bible-pusher is excited at the prospect of receiving the distinguished award of a rhinoceros mascot statue branded Schwarzkopf. But somebody else showed eight. She's disappointed at her loss. "There's always next week," I console her. "Are you mocking me?" She asks. "No," I tell her, "this has been real inspirational, It reminds me of that Catholic Charismatic healing revival you took me to the last time I was in town." The next day we're driving seventy-miles-an-hour down the expressway towards the city. I casually mention my future plans to visit South Dakota and renew relatives' acquaintances. But I want to steer clear of the giant ashtray situated in the Black Hills. "Why?" She asks me. "Because I don't like it when my mascara smears." I gingerly explain. She then attempts to enlighten me with old-glory-sermons about how Mount Rushmore is a beautiful homage and tribute to America's great forefathers and she doesn't blame me for getting all misty-eyed at the sight of such a heavenly and magnificent structure. She's talking about it as if it's one of the ten great natural wonders of the world. "No," I tell her. "It's not *that* way, you don't get it. It's a desecration of sacred land. It's a monument erected that symbolizes the near-destruction of a conquered people." My argument doesn't

68

faze her, she's steadfast in her conviction, and begins to passionately further her cause by explaining that it's too bad what happened in history and all but the past is the past and that *we* should all just get on with it. I want to scream savagely, *WHAT DO YOU MEAN WE, WHAT DO YOU MEAN WE!* I want to jump out of her Mercedes for a Geronimo landing off the edge of the world to the tune of *Gonna Fly Now.* But instead, I remain stoic. I'm not a converter, evangelist or missionary. But later I wrote her an un-mailed letter.

Dear _____,

When you told me that you thought we should all just forget about the past and not be embittered by it and learn to get along, I don't think you realized that you were simplifying an amazingly horrible part of American history. You're explanation would be like telling a black person that slavery was kind of a rotten thing and all but that it really did great things for the south. Or would you ever imagine explaining to a Jewish person that the Holocaust was just a necessary tactic for the empowerment of the Third Reich? Why is there no perspective? I think these things are all relatively equatable. How's your business by the way? Found any new cultists? Have you won the Schwarzkopf rhino mascot yet? Do you still think that the Gulf War was a good idea? I can't help but wonder if your associate business members are the same folks that are lobbying for the inclusion of Ronald Reagan in the Mount Rushmore "shrine."

In regret and disbelief, your friend,

Tiffany

7.

My friend Rob and I are grazing on french fries and burger deluxes outside Dick's Drive-Up restaurant on Capital Hill when an anonymous man distracts us from our grease-treat consumption with certain interrogative imperatives ending with question marks. "Do you know Jesus?" He asks. "Jesus Garcia? Yeah, he's my friend's brother." I reply. "No, no, I mean Jesus Christ," he explains, "do you have a personal relationship with Jesus Christ?" I tell him, "Well, I tried for awhile but he never returned my phone messages." "Would you like to?" The stranger asks. "Like to *what?*" I return. "Would you like to have a personal relationship with Jesus Christ?" "No, that's OK," I tell him, "I'm spiritually intact." "What, what!?" He flounders, "I'm not trying to attack you, what makes you think I'm trying to attack you!?" "In-tact, in-tact," I reassure him, "I'm spiritually *in-tact.*" "Oh." He says and pauses. "Do you want a personal relationship with Jesus Christ?" "No, that's OK," I tell him, "he's not my type."

8.

If you find yourself driving the stretch of highway between Wolf Point and Poplar Montana, beware of the Boy-
With-No-Eyes. He's not a roadside prophet. He's not a
thousand year old soul who channels the minds and bodies of bored housewives. He's not a road sign signaling the
last 500 years of *Gas Food Lodging.* He's a 20th Century
legend hitching his way into the next millennium. The
highway crosses explain his cryptic tricks played on lonely
travelers driving at night. My cousin Wayne in '91 flew out
of his truck window and arrived broken into the next
world. The Boy-With-No-Eyes assisted him into the House
of Spirits. Eliza, back in '62 failed in her vision and ca-
reened head-on into an oncoming semi. The Boy-With-
No-Eyes led her way into the Happy Hunting Grounds.
Silas Tail Spins, Ruby No Blankets, Esther Spotted Bird,
met the End of their Trail on Highway 2, fell into the mys-
terious mouth of death, and the Boy-With-No-Eyes waved
them down into the day after tomorrow.

9.

Today is only a sequel from yesterday. Tomorrow is the upcoming episode we'll be sure not to miss.

10.

Driving across Highway 212, straight into the heart of Crow Country, straight into the pulse of a historian's Wonderland, straight into bluffs and valleys of stained battlegrounds, straight into a field of one glorious and necessary victory, on one glorious yesterday. Driving across Highway 212 you can't miss the Custer Battlefield National Monument. The only monument in America named for the loser. Go figure? The name may have been changed to the Little Bighorn Battlefield, but the honorable vigil to the 7th Cavalry still remains ignited in the majority of America's mainstream. After-all Custer died for our sins right? Along the tour, among the grave sites and headstones are signs that heed—

Warning:
Beware of rattlesnakes

And beyond those signs are others. Spoken in the softest and most ancient of whispers. Carried by the furious wind that blows forever across the wide sea of prairie, the big sky of endless horizon. Whispers carried along the eternity of flowing waters—

Warning:
Beware of ghosts

Rodeo Queen

*"Let any normally healthy woman who is
ordinarily strong screw up her courage and tackle
a bucking bronco and she will find the most
fascinating pastime in the field of feminine
athletic endeavor. There is nothing to compare to
increase the joy of living, and once accomplished,
she'll have more real fun than any pink tea or
theater party or ballroom ever yielded."*

—May Lillie

Publicists and newspaper folk like to call us equestrienne
beauties of the prairie, pretty girls
on horses, daring flowers of the west.
But we are more than all that, more than lean
bodies, frilly petticoats, bloomers and chaps,
we are a prized attraction, rugged rodeo stars!

First of all, this job takes an iron constitution
and sheer grit, why if we had our way in the real
world, we'd be bankers or presidents, the best
of 'em too, but I have been
in that other world and I'll be no sap
playing the role of "proper lady"—not even on a dare!

I can't think of any better occupation
than roper and rider, no better fulfill-
ment than taming a wild bronco that tests
my courage or a big mean
bull that knocks the wind out'a my sails, slams me flat
on my back, proclaiming a war!

To our fellow women and mothers who question
our rare appetites, I say I don't care that my curls

get dusty, my hands get callused or my skirts get messed.
You can say I'm odd, strange or obscene,
but in my ten-gallon hat
I'm bigger than life, I'll smoke if I want, even go in a bar!

Forget your rules and tradition,
your social teas, religion and pearl
colored linens, I ain't like all the rest
of your sisters, 'cuz I'm a rodeo queen,
a cowgirl, a bulldogger. Whatever propriety I lack
is your problem, 'cuz I always knew that I'd go far!

Outlaws, Renegades & Saints

He could've been a product of righteous stock, a son
who turned his mama's milk sour. One who lived
by a badland's philosophy, whose heart spilled wild
blood against the brow of a saint, a savage, an outlaw,
stealer of horses, bearer of iron-barreled arms
and steel knives. He was the legend who shot a man

down just for snoring. He could be the man
branded as the frontier demon, who rose after the sun
set, who dropped to his knees into the arms
of Satan himself, who bartered his life
for immortality, who chased after crooked dreams and law-
less trails into the dawn of the *Wild Wild*

West. He could've been raised by wild
beasts, weaned by wolves or women
of ill-repute. He could be the in-law
who stole your daughter, he could be your son.
He could take your sacred life's
breath and extinguish it in his strangling arms,

or shape widows from the lead of his firearms,
form their tears into dust and laugh at their wild
screams for mercy. **Wanted Dead or Alive**
posters line post-office walls, Law-men
with hats so big they block the sun
quote prices for the head of an outlaw.

A criminal has many names. An outlaw
could be a renegade, or even a saint waiting for armageddon, waiting for the Father, Son
or Holy Ghost to save him from wild-
fires of hell/damnation where a man
could burn for eternity, where devils live

and condemned spirits dwell. Such a life
on earth is forbidden to enter a perfect law-
abiding heaven. Imagine it, men
in golden robes walking arm and arm
among the clouds, beyond the wild-
nerness, the carved horizons of blazing sun.

There are legends of evil reformed, of outlaws
turned saint in arms of angels. Oh pray the wild
ice hearts of such men will melt under merciful suns.

Even The Outlaw's Daughter Get's The Blues

One: I Dreamt You Were The High Plains Drifter

I woke from a bad b-grade dream.
               Some old western blazed across
my mind's screen playing the sound-
               track of my life. *(Boom-boom-boom*
boom-boom-boom-boom-boom-
               boom-boom) You were riding
high against the backdrop, pistols
               hung low on your hips
and a stogie balanced with the grace
               of a two-pack-a-day-habit
flavored your non-grinning lips. The camera
               rolled to the landscape
beyond, centered on the posse closing
               in behind the dust kicked
up by your horse's hooves. All white
               steeds chased you against
a red-canyon wall and shot
               you down. Blood splashed my picture
in horrific black and white as you fell
               over a deep clay cliff screaming

GERRROOOOOOONIMOOOOOOOOOO!

Every outlaw I know is a warrior,
               every warrior an outlaw, especially
faced with the bitter, sweet, end.

Two: Scene From The Outlaw's Trail Of Tears

(Action)
I wander the interstate hitching for a ride anywhere
    but here. Anywhere
but from where I've just come—-anywhere
    but the place
I fear I might be heading. If anywhere
    were a motel,
let's say, it would have a blue and green marquee
    flashing *ANYWHERE*
MOTEL: THE PLACE YOU WANT TO BE.

(Scene 2)
I'd go in, lay down, hug a pillow to my heart, escape into
    the borders of yesterday,
retrace every step of the outlaw's trail, follow the
    footprints he left behind.

(Flashback)
Dream twisted versions of once-upon-a-time, the story
    about the misunderstood
prince who kidnapped the little princess, the story about
    holding her for ransom,
the story where he stole her for a bounty of gold, delivered
    her to the reservation
of his own design, the story about trading her for the fabric
    of a worn-out marriage.

(Cut To)
The Happy Ending. I'm still waiting for the happy ending.
    Still traveling the interstate
delirious thumb to asphalt waiting for the outlaw's return,
    still mailing letters C/O
Outlaw Avenue, country of tropical paradise, Gaugin's
    refuge, Friday's fugitive island,
Coconut Dream Cream Drive where palm trees line the
    streets and hillsides like soldiers,

where exotic women in spandex hotpants will grant you
    anything for a dollar, *anything*
to help you escape from the exact place your mind takes
    you, *anything*
to make you forget the places where you've been, *anything*
    to stop reminding
you of the places you fear you might be heading.
    Anything. **(Cut)**

Three: The Good The Bad And The Ugly

————My father tells me, *"Life ain't no Hollywood western where the bad   guy is all bad and the good guy all good, 'cept Clint Eastwood. Now if he were a color, he'd be grey. Always remember, only zebras come in black and white."*
————After he extends this unique piece of wisdom, I disregard every color in my crayon box and use only grey to fill in between the lines. Later, my teacher calls to inquire, *"Is everything alright at home?"*
————My mother tells her, *"Everything is fine, just great."*
————But all I hear is, *everything is grey—everything is grey—everything is grey.*

Four: The Outlaw's Last Stand

My father was in college the first
time FBI agents hunted him down.
While giving an anti-war speech

in protest to the Unites States'
involvement in Southeast Asia,
he accentuated his point of view

by setting a match to his draft-
card & his classmates applauded
as the room filled with smoke

detonating the sprinkler system.
Showers of water fell like napalm,
like Saigon. *God it was beautiful.*

In the movies outlaws always turn
into heroes. Bad becomes saintly
& ugliness transcends any foul deed,

any pock-marked or beautiful dream.
Water exploding...so fuckin' beautiful.
My father's stunt failed to land him

in jail, (he'd only burned an old issue)
I'd say he was lucky not fighting
in Asia, but irony works strange

magic. Because years later
he ducked the feds & fled to that one
place he'd hoped to avoid,

that one day while making his first
defiant stand with fire. His premier
outlaw gesture to a society that

only wanted to contort, twist & hang
him eventually. *So beautiful . . .*
so goddamn fuckin' beautiful.

Five: A Japanese Cowgirl Gets The Blues

I never told you what happened that night you and
Chikako were captured at the Canadian border. Like Bon-
nie and Clyde, like Belle Starr and Jim July, like Wild

Bill and Calamity Jane. That night we fled to catch a moment's glimpse of the face we hadn't seen for too many
years to imagine. On the phone you kept asking, *why*

so calm, so indifferent? Almost as if indifference elevated
my character. It's funny in retrospect, in the way that com-
edy is tragedy plus time, you know? Did I ever

tell you about that night? How I drank an entire pint of
Jack Daniels straight-up, to somehow numb out the pain
of knowing you were back in the country,

to somehow defeat all those anxiety demons circling
around me like too many bad memories, too many stale
and powerless dreams. I puked all the way home

and Chikako held my head and patted my shoulders and
after I was finished with every last cold shudder, Chikako
began to cry silent polite tears and I smoothed

her straight black hair and patted her small thin shoulders, murmuring in English words she couldn't understand, translated, *it's OK.* She expected Disneyland

and the Grand Canyon and all she ever got was a one-way
ticket to nightmare city. Did I ever tell you about that
night? Did I ever tell you about the next day? How

Chikako and I went for a long walk down Pacific Highway
South and got lost? How we took a detour through Seatac
Airport and fell into the lap of Alice's

Wonderland? We wandered the parking lots and terminal entrances, climbed over gates and barbedwire fences and along a lush green lawn found a storybook picture

complete with magic, fairy dust and a happy ending. We were greeted by a school of thick-stemmed toadstools, large as mayo-jars with round red lids speckled with

polka-dots. They were sitting there waiting for us, waiting for us to find them, and they greeted us, as if to say, *you've just entered the twilight zone.* Greeted us

as if to say, *Dr. Suess says take two of these and call me in the morning.*
Did I ever tell you that story?

Six: The Lullaby You Taught Me
To Sing In E Minor

i imagine that i'm dreaming
somebody else's dream where

in the exact moment before
i wake up i touch you

& witness your face exploding
sending out sparks

extravagant as japanese fireworks
magnificent as asteroids

elegant as bone china breaking
& every dream ends the same

revolves around & around
like angry circling planets with

too much magic to spend
blossoms of chaos the brilliance

of dark petals expands infinitely
within the universe & rests

in the shade of your thoughts
thoughts i can't capture

thoughts that curl & flutter
spin & fall against the cold tile

of our separation
some dreams you never wake up from

Seven: The Eternal Wait For A Happy Ending

I try to laugh at pain as if it were a sacred clown painted in black and white stripes performing stunts on the trapeze of someone else's tragedy. Laughter is the medicine administered like communion wafers to the good, the bad and the ugly. When I conjure up the old wounds inflicted by those years you spent incarcerated, I think first of those earlier times you made me laugh. Those evenings when you wrapped me in my bed covers like a mummy and promised that I was a cocoon now, but in the morning I would be a butterfly. Or those nights when I would steal out of bed and discover you in a sanctuary of three-in-the-morning-blues, wrapping your jaws around pickle and peanut butter sandwiches. Or the time we played an impromptu game of hide-and-go-seek, and we looked everywhere for you, under the beds, in the closets, behind the curtains, but couldn't find you until morning when you emerged from sleeping in the cherry tree. I refuse to discard those memories. I refuse to discard you. The parts of yourself you left behind. The parts you've been searching for all these years and failed to locate have been with me all this time waiting for your claim ticket. Waiting to forgive you and call you home. Waiting for the happy ending we're all born to live, born to deserve. I want you to know that forgiveness hasn't any price higher than you can afford. I want you to know that a happy ending doesn't just exist in the dreams we never wake up from. I want you to know that courage multiplied by forgiveness equals an unending promise to an exponential power. I want you to know that every story doesn't have to take this long to tell, when what you really mean to say in the shortest possible way is I love you. *I love you.*

Reward

Wanted
Dead or Alive
trickster fugitive
responsible
for flash flood, hurricane, earthquake
&
end of the millennium hysteria
armed with
craft & cunning
considered dangerous
exercise extreme caution
fugitive
has many disguises
known alias' include
spider, coyote, rabbit, raven
political candidate
&
used car salesman
any information leading to fugitive's arrest
will be awarded
in the amount of
immortality

FOUR

The Reflection of Reluctant Saints

She Speaks Her Many Tongues

————Sunday arrived seven-days-a-week at Grandmother Iron Thunder's house. Religion flew in through the windows like flocks of white doves scavenging for communion crumbs. With the rising of every sun my grandmother's tongue began its eternal lashing at anything that wasn't holy.

————*You will one day kneel before the lord in judgment.* She preached over Quaker Oats and toast. *Your mother may perish with the wicked but Jesus has a special plan for you.*

————In church Pastor Johnson shook his fists towards the North Dakota sky, sweat running into his eyes, bellowing out strange and exotic words. The congregation waved their hands in the air, crying to be so blessed, crying to be so saved, crying to be so devout. The chapel hummed with the voices, harmonies echoed through every pew, collected beneath the floor-boards. The music invaded my bones, planted itself as a solid thing and refused to leave like an impolite guest.

————Grandmother Iron Thunder jabbed my side. *Go and be saved daughter.* She pushed me toward the pulpit where Pastor Johnson shook imaginary tears of Christ into my face. *Accept Jesus into your heart child—hear him knocking—let him in today and forever—let me hear you now—I love you Jesus!*

————For the next several weeks I pretended I was saved. When Pastor Johnson and his plain wife came calling, I feigned thrill with their gift of homemade salami and chokecherry preserves. Pastor Johnson nestled his stocky frame into the cushions of the davenport, replied a loud and hearty affirmation when Grandmother offered them tea. I slunk into the kitchen to heat the kettle listening in on their living-room conversation.

————*Brother Lloyd was a good man.* Said Pastor Johnson. *We sure do miss him in bible study.*

————*I miss him too.* grandmother said. *Seems not a moment goes by that I don't think of him.*

————*Death isn't a finality but a homecoming.* Pastor Johnson said.

————*Yes, of course, a return to our lord.* Grandmother said.

————*Amen.* The Pastor's wife murmured.

Saints

—For my mother

I. Eliza

The call arrived after midnight.
Come and collect this child,
the voice murmured like a black defeat.
My stepdaughter Ethel gave birth
in a one-room cabin in Bullhead South Dakota.
Through nine months of pregnancy
she hoarded a child in her belly,
disguised it in pastel-flowered shifts,
hid her sin from God and the neighbors,
concealed her dirty little secret.
But for us her disowned was a shining jewel,
the child we were too old to conceive,
and we loved her.
My present husband proved to be my savior.
All those wasted years I spent with Ethel's father,
being the dutiful wife, bearing the fury
of his iron fists and cruel words.
I raised you in his house Ethel.
I gave you warm praises,
sewed and washed your dresses,
cooked your food.
You were more than a stepdaughter to me,
I loved you as my own. Now
you offer me this gift of your body.
This child that addresses your shame.
This child you will abandon.
This child you will not love.
Yes Ethel, I will raise my grandchild,
I will give her all that you cannot.

I will take her to the Catholic Church,
I will quiz her lessons,
I will see that she is baptized.
Your sin will never own her.
God and the neighbors will forgive you.
I forgive you Ethel.

11. Ethel

My body burst open near midnight.
I thought my bones were on fire.
I cried out against the pain,
imagined my soul was leaving me.
Forgive me, forgive me!
I ranted in an explosion of fever.
The child poured out from between my legs,
entering into the world, issued
a scream I knew was accusation.
I would not hold you,
forgive me.
I would not feed you,
forgive me.
I would not even look at you,
forgive me.
I will give you to Eliza and Richard.
This is the best I can do.
This is all I can do.
Please do not hate me child.
Nights after your departure,
I will stare wildly into the stars,
kneel at Mary's feet,
count out my rosaries for every prayer,
and seek my atonement.
I tell myself, with time my ache
will lessen. You will erase yourself
from my soul's grasp.
I will marry a good man,

birth other daughters,
ones I can keep, ones I can cherish,
not in secrecy and shame,
but out in the open,
before the whole world,
before God.

111. Alita Rose

The dark woman arrives on my birthday.
She gives me gifts of dresses and ribbons.
Tempts me with candy Lent won't allow
me to take. She makes me call her *Mama*,
wants to hold me in her tight perfumed arms.
But I run out of the house,
flee to the river,
release a torrent of tears I don't understand.
The woman stays for two long days.
All-the-time pleading with my mother,
Let me take her she is mine!
But my mother ignores her,
clamps her jaw and narrows her eyes.
The woman begins to cry,
But I am her mother!
Then she reaches to snatch me,
my father holds me close to his chest,
shakes his head sadly and tells her,
You must go, Alita stays here.
The woman walks out the door,
she doesn't say goodbye.
My mother gives back the dresses
and ribbons, they embrace on the porch.
In confession I ask the priest for forgiveness,
for making this woman so sad.
He tells me, it is not I that needs
forgiveness, it is I who needs
to forgive.

Iron Eyes Cody

An Indian famous for his rainwater eyes
blazed through Wolf Point Main in a shiny white Cadillac.
Smiling and waving like President Nixon,
tossing Tootsie Pops like the Pope might toss rosaries.
Brown skinned kids snatching a little of their own
Independence Day glory,
congregated the street, abandoned their mothers,
fled toward the famous Indian seen on TV.

All of my life the planet has cried for a savior.
My grandmothers ensure their P.O. boxes in heaven,
spend their last few years preaching me the gospel,
their mouths deliver a tongue of living testimony,
proof that their grandmothers prayed to the wrong spirit.

Who was Black Elk? Who was Wovoka?

Armageddon lays heavy in the tallest of steeples,
in the grandest of state capital suites,
in the smoke that curls around an old one's pipe.

Iron Eyes Cody consecrated my first communion,
on the day America celebrated liberty from a monarch,
during a year when a war was being forgotten,
in a time when TV was more important
than kings,
than grandmothers,
than preachers and prophets,
than politicians,
than real Indians.

Godless Nights & Firewater

Before Mavis June found religion in a church pew, she did her communion with whiskey sours. We were all sleeping the night she poured through the screen door at three-in-the-morning, alcohol boiling her blood, firewater singing through her tongue. She came home fixin' to lacerate/berate/downrate her *no-good-account* sons. Hissing & squawking she broke the bread of night, after the lightning came the flood, the red sea of her opened & Mavis June evicted us with her tears. During our next visit, we were introduced to a sober Mavis June. *I looked to the gray gray sky & Christ was crying!* She said. Grandma Iron Thunder, dark & devout exclaimed, *Praise Jesus!* Grandma Wing dropped fry bread dough into the oil, sang, *Amen!* The next day Mavis June took me to the rehab clinic where she was employed as a secretary. I shot pool with Davis Long Hair. He'd since graduated from the withdrawal & deetees program. His diploma was a pool stick that didn't shake & clear fluid eyes. Eyes that followed mine, teased my 8-ball to glide into the corner pocket. 2 nights later, I spotted him at the Oil-Celebration Powwow, his hand linked with a homely Indian girl's. When I asked, Mavis June explained that he left the clinic, went back to his drinking life. *The Lord will find him.* She said.

Recipe For Survival

*—Dedicated to Charity Wing
and the sons and daughters*

First the woman cuts the red and marbled meat,
once part of a humming beat of deer,
which a good neighbor shot and brought to her.
During the depression years, her husband
also used to track and hunt to fill the bellies
of his family, those five hungry brown faced runts,
whose youth at times demanded harsh punishments.
But they revered and inherited faith of God and grew
tall and strong as straw; *in the beginning.*

Then the onion fumes are felt and the woman swipes
a swelling finger across her wrinkled cheek.
The knife she uses slices pieces of wild turnips,
corn and carrots for her plain stew and in the government built kitchen she prowls a mouse
chewing on an oatmeal grain dropped and the tender
mouse scurries under a wood panel to an unknown
place as the woman sweeps it away with her broom,
recalling her dearest son.

The son whose contagious laughter used to shake
the rooms the family squeezed into and much later
with his young wife and baby daughter, during one
terrible autumn, he fell from his family's hands, his
family's tree, into the hands of his maker. Still
the woman cuts vegetables for her lineage soup.
Year after year, *the good son is dead.*

The woman becomes active in a ladies church
organization, only quits after gossip breeds from tears
and during that winter her daughter shrank
from a stroke and gripped tightly
onto an unknown life like a child to a doll,
while needles pricked her lifeless skin and cold metal
enveloped her sterile bed. The woman was seventy
then and her daughter barely forty, waited in a nursing
home while the nurses commented, *what irony.*

In bringing life and offering nourishment to her plain
stew, the woman pours the meat into the pot,
where it steams, cooks, boils the water
into a necessary broth. The vegetables
waiting on the counter for their cooking
time, sit blind and still, soon be eaten.
A grandchild peeks her bright cheeks into the kitchen
and the woman leans down to receive a morning kiss.

The Poet as Messiah

this is a poem that will save the world
this is a poem that will save the world
this is a poem that will save the world
this is a poem that will save the world
this is a poem that will save the world
this is a poem that will save the world
this is a poem that will save the world
this is a poem that will save the world
this is a poem that will save the world
this is a poem that will save the world
this is a poem that will save the world this is a poem that will save the world
this is a poem that will save the world this is a poem that will save the world
this is a poem that will save the world this is a poem that will save the world
this is a poem that will save the world this is a poem that will save the world
this is a poem that will save the world this is a poem that will save the world
this is a poem that will save the world this is a poem that will save the world
this is a poem that will save the world this is a poem that will save the world
this is a poem that will save the world this is a poem that will save the world
this is a poem that will save the world this is a poem that will save the world
this is a poem that will save the world
this is a poem that will save the world
this is a poem that will save the world
this is a poem that will save the world
this is a poem that will save the world
this is a poem that will save the world
this is a poem that will save the world
this is a poem that will save the world
this is a poem that will save the world
this is a poem that will save the world
this is a poem that will save the world
this is a poem that will save the world
this is a poem that will save the world
this is a poem that will save the world
this is a poem that will save the world
this is a poem that will save the world
this is a poem that will save the world

Night Of The Living Dead

—For Sherman Alexie

"If they come back from the dead, will they be our friends?
Or our enemies? Will we be able to deal with them? We who
have never conquered our fear of confronting death."
      —John Russo, *Night of the Living Dead* (1974)

Resurrected
from coffins and vaults,
the recent and not-so-recent deceased
had risen
armed with their own baggage of testimony
to tell.

I've failed to escape the certain horror of this picture.
The inconsolable image the b-movie inflicted.
Some twenty years later I find myself asking—

what if?

What if the ghost dancers at Wounded Knee
were to rise from their mass grave
and turn the world upside-down?
Suppose delirious prophesies came true.

What then?

Tell me, how is forgiveness possible
with so many reasons for revenge?
In a time when the most accessible cliche',
the best revenge is living well,
so cruelly mocks the fate of today's Indian.

This is what happens when massacres
become just another metaphor.

The bones of the dead
are excavated, scattered, sold.
Shrines are blasted from sacred
rock in the name of patriotism.

Lakota religion is stolen by goofy mystics
peddling crystals and incense.
Cherokee becomes just another brand
for affordable clothing and 4x4s.

A magnificent past is reduced to hallmark
cards postmarked galaxies away.

If you listen,
if you listen *hard,*
it is possible to eavesdrop on the dead.
Don't you know?
They have been talking for years.
Their spirits are still dancing
telling the same story over and over.

Their voices are overheard by TV evangelists
and talk-show hosts.
Their voices spill into city water systems,
their voices fill the emptiest places in the universe—
in the bottoms of swimming pools,
in the dead ends of lonely streets,
in old fears wrapped in wet blankets,
in unclean thoughts in dull knives in stale dreams

can you hear them?

Every generation of every society of every culture
manufactures its own savior.
To be saved to be saved to be saved

is an expression used to halt our own destruction.
To save ourselves from ourselves. From—

artillery   ambush   Armageddon   anguish
from—
gunpowder   angry gods   germicide   early graves
from—
the past   the present   the future   from—

lives, lives, lives. *These are our lives.*
Why didn't the soldiers hear the dead talking?

In Laguna territory a Pueblo woman roasts
pinon nuts as offering to her dead relatives' graves.
Her body ignites long candles and melts into spirit.
Her children parade as goblins through the brilliant night,
set fire to their shadows, pinch food from their bowls
to feed to the dead. *They hear the dead talking.*

The night I witnessed
John Russo's script-come-to-life,
grotesque grade-b flic,
I was amazed and astounded.
By the end of the drama
its message bled bright red
through my thoughts,
staked its claim on my heart,
because *I heard.*

The screen only offered a black and white
view but every zombie was technicolor green,
every victim's flesh bloomed bright purple and blue.

I heard the dead talking.

Every life extinguished re-invents itself to another form.
This was the message,
a warning that the dead are always alive.

In a world where every generation
of every society of every culture designs
its own messianic hysteria,
where hope can shatter like glass
and a people's dream can perish

so violently,

the ghosts will always be with us.
Listening and watching.
Carrying our burdens on their backs,
appearing in our visions,
announcing themselves at the cinema,
on satellite TV, in the wires and coils,
in the basements and cupboards,

always,

they will be with us, declaring themselves
at Hollywood premiers, every inaugural ball,
in the cyberspace highways, in the quiet of night,

waltzing our nightmares to sleep,
preserving our faith in tomorrow—

listen,

can you hear the dead talking?
They are saving and resurrecting us all.

First Book Awards For Poetry

Established in 1992 in conjunction with the Returning The Gift Festival, The North American Native Authors Poetry Award is given for a first book by a Native writer. Named the Diane Decorah Award in memory of a Native writer and supporter of other Native authors, its winners published by The Greenview Review Press are:

1992   Gloria Bird *Full Moon On The Reservation*

1993   Kimberly Blaeser *Trailing You*

1994   Tiffany Midge *Outlaws, Renegades and Saints*

1995   Denise Sweet *Songs For Discharming*